Erato and His Sieve

by A. I. Freeman

illustrated by Wendy Born Hollander

HOUGHTON MIFFLIN   BOSTON

Printed in China

ISBN 10: 0-618-89891-3
ISBN 13: 978-0-618-89891-6

56789   0940   16 15 14 13 12
4500356275

Eratosthenes' Achievements

Eratosthenes was a man of many interests. He was born in 276 B.C. in Cyrene, in North Africa. Eratosthenes began his learning in Cyrene. Then he went to Athens, Greece, to study under great teachers.

Ptolemy III, the king of Egypt, noticed him. The king asked Eratosthenes to go to Alexandria to tutor his son. Before long, Eratosthenes became the head of the Library of Alexandria. He spent the rest of his life in the city.

Eratosthenes wrote a book about geometry.

He made a list of all the known stars.

He measured the distance of the Sun and Moon from Earth.

He measured Earth's tilt.

He worked on a calendar that included leap years.

He wrote long poems.

Eratosthenes did all this and more, but he is best remembered for two things.

Eratosthenes is best remembered for measuring Earth and showing that it is round. His measurement was very close to the actual size of Earth.

He is also remembered for his sieve of prime numbers. A sieve is a strainer. It has tiny holes or a screen. Big things stay on top of the screen and smaller things fall through. It separates by size. Eratosthenes' sieve didn't separate by size, but it did separate different kinds of numbers. Let's see how it works.

Read·Think·Write For which two things is Eratosthenes best remembered?

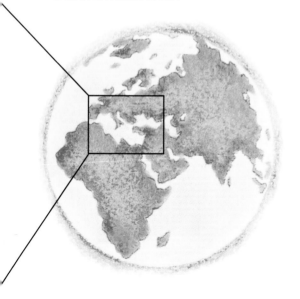

Eratosthenes thought that Earth was round. He even measured it!

Prime and Composite Numbers

A prime number is a whole number that has only itself and 1 as factors. Here are some examples:

The number 2 is a prime number. It has only itself and 1 as factors.

The number 3 is a prime number. It has only itself and 1 as factors.

The number 11 is a prime number. It has only itself and 1 as factors.

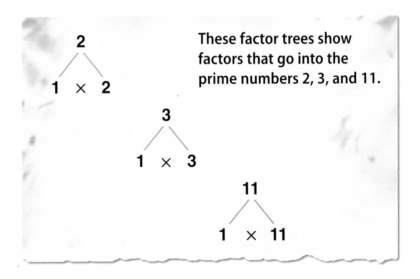

These factor trees show factors that go into the prime numbers 2, 3, and 11.

Read·Think·Write Why is 5 a prime number? Is 7 a prime number? Why?

A composite number is a whole number that has more than two factors. The number 4 is a composite number, because it has the factors, 1, 2, and 4.

Except for 2, all even numbers are composite numbers. Do you know why? The number 2 is a factor for all even numbers, such as 4, 6, 8, and so on. So, all even numbers other than 2 have at least three factors.

Odd numbers can be composite numbers, too. For example, the factors of 9 are 1, 3, and 9. The factors of 15 are 1, 3, 5, and 15.

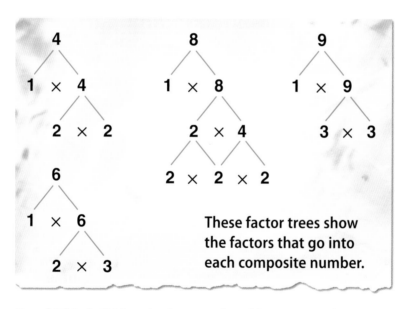

These factor trees show the factors that go into each composite number.

Read·Think·Write Is the number 10 a composite number? Why?

The Sieve of Eratosthenes

Eratosthenes wanted an easy way to figure out prime numbers. First, he wrote out a list of numbers. He crossed out 1. The number 1 is neither a prime nor a composite number. It only has one factor.

Then he circled 2 because it's a prime number. He crossed out all the other even numbers because 2 is a factor of all even numbers.

Next, he circled the prime number 3. Then he crossed out all the odd numbers that 3 is a factor of. The even numbers that 3 is a factor of had already been crossed out.

Read·Think·Write What are three composite numbers that 3 is a factor of that Eratosthenes would have crossed out next?

COMPOSITE NUMBERS

PRIME NUMBERS

1̶	2	3	4̶	5	6̶	7	8̶	9̶	10̶
11	12̶	13	14̶	15̶	16̶	17	18̶	19	20̶
21̶	22̶	23	24̶	25̶	26̶	27̶	28̶	29	30̶
31	32̶	33̶	34̶	35̶	36̶	37	38̶	39̶	40̶
41	42̶	43	44̶	45̶	46̶	47	48̶	49̶	50̶

When Eratosthenes had crossed out all the numbers that 3 is a factor of, he moved on to 4. He didn't have to cross out any numbers. Do you know why? The number 4 is an even number. The number 4 can be divided by 2. So, any number that can be divided by 4 is an even number that had already been crossed out.

Eratosthenes continued on to number 5. He crossed out numbers that 5 is a factor of. If you know how to count by fives, this is an easy one. He crossed out any number that 5 is a factor of that hadn't already been crossed out. That means he crossed out 25, 35, and 45. Eratosthenes continued in this way to make his sieve.

People are still working on finding new prime numbers. Today we can use computers to help sieve big, long prime numbers.

Read·Think·Write After 5, what number did Eratosthenes circle next? Then what numbers did he cross out?

1. What happens if you multiply any prime number by the prime number 2?

2. What happens if you multiply any prime number by the prime number 5?

3. What happens if you multiply any prime number by the composite number 4?

4. Which of these is a composite number, 71 or 81?

5. What is the next prime number over 100?

Activity

Draw Conclusions Work with a partner to discuss these questions. Use the table on page 7 to help you.

- How can you describe prime numbers?
- In what kind of order are the prime numbers?
- How do you know that the number 18 is not a prime number?
- How can you tell that the number 37 is a prime number?
- What can you say that describes all composite numbers?